Phillis Wheatley

Heroes of the American Revolution

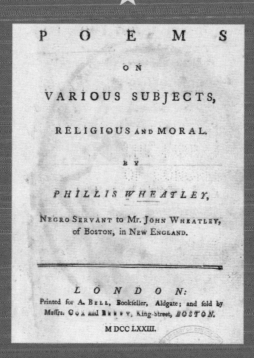

Don McLeese

Rourke
Publishing LLC
Vero Beach, Florida 32964

www.rourkepublishing.com

PHOTO CREDITS: Covers, Title page, pages 6, 9, 19, 24, 28©Getty Images; Pages 4, 5, 10, 13, 14, 16, 20, 26 ©North Wind Picture Archives; Pages 23, 27 from the Library of Congress

Title page: *The cover of the elegy written by Phillis Wheatley*

Editor: Frank Sloan

Cover and page design by Nicola Stratford

Library of Congress Cataloging-in-Publication Data

McLeese, Don.
  Phillis Wheatley / Don McLeese.
     p. cm. -- (Heroes of the American revolution)
  Includes bibliographical references and index.
  ISBN 1-59515-220-2 (hard cover)
  1. Wheatley, Phillis, 1753-1784--Juvenile literature. 2. Poets, American--Colonial period, ca. 1600-1775--Biography--Juvenile literature. 3. Slaves--United States--Biography--Juvenile literature. 4. African American poets--Biography--Juvenile literature. I. Title. II. Series: McLeese, Don. Heroes of the American Revolution.
  PS866.W5Z655 2004
  811'.1--dc22   2004007609

Printed in the USA

LB/LB

Table of Contents

★

An Amazing Woman 4

Born in Africa 8

Sold into Slavery 11

On the Slave Ship 12

Slave Auction 15

The Wheatleys 17

Letting Her Learn 18

The Poems of Phillis Wheatley 21

Published in London 25

A Free Woman 26

Her Poetry Lives On 29

Time Line 30

Glossary 31

Index 32

Further Reading/Websites to Visit 32

An Amazing Woman

★

During the period of the Revolutionary War, there was no more amazing woman who lived in America than Phillis Wheatley. At this time, learning to read and write wasn't considered nearly as important for a woman as it was for a man.

African Americans, both women and men, rarely went to school. Most of them were slaves, owned by white people. Slaves had to work without being paid and did whatever their white owners told them to do.

Slaves in their quarters during the 1700s

Slaves process cotton in the American South.

POEMS

ON

VARIOUS SUBJECTS,

RELIGIOUS AND MORAL.

BY

PHILLIS WHEATLEY,

NEGRO SERVANT to Mr. JOHN WHEATLEY,
of BOSTON, in NEW ENGLAND.

The title page of Phillis Wheatley's major book of poems

As an African-American girl, Phillis not only knew how to read and write, but she also learned to write **poetry**. Everyone who read what she wrote thought that Phillis was a great poet, one whose poems should be published in a book. In 1773, when Phillis was just 20 years old, her poems were collected into a book titled *Poems on Various Subjects, Religious and Moral.*

This book not only made her the first important black poet but also the first African American ever to have her writing published. She showed that a slave could not only be a good worker, but also a great writer.

Born in Africa

★

Phillis was born in 1753 in West Africa, probably in the country called Senegal. Africa is a long way across the ocean from America. We don't know the exact date of her birthday, which is now celebrated on July 11. We don't even know what her name was when she lived in Africa. She wasn't given the name Phillis Wheatley until she came to America.

AFRICA

Africa is a large **continent** across the Atlantic Ocean from America. Many of the people who live there have darker skins than people who come from Europe. Darker-skinned people who live in the United States are often known as African Americans.

～

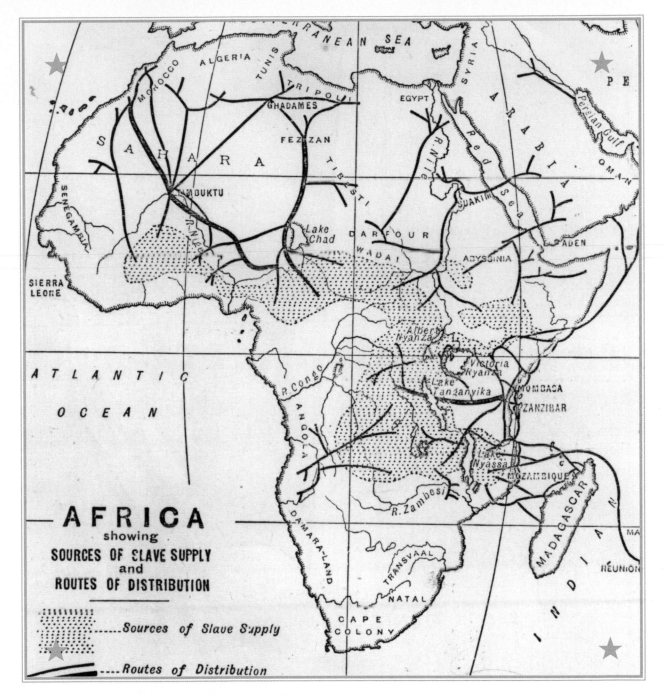

This map of Africa shows slave routes.

Slaves were captured and marched to be sold.

Sold into Slavery

---★---

When Phillis was just a little girl of seven, she was taken away from her home in Africa. She was **kidnapped** and put on a boat to America to be sold as a slave. At that time, black people from Africa could be owned by white people in America. Today, we know that no person should own another person, that every person should be free. But to those who took Phillis, this seven-year-old girl had no more rights than an animal or even a piece of furniture. She could be bought and sold.

SLAVERY

Slavery became illegal in the United States in 1865, after the Civil War between the states in the north (which were against slavery) and the states in the south (which were for it). Today, slavery is against the law in practically every country.

~

On the Slave Ship

★

A ship took Phillis and other Africans who had been captured to America. This trip on the seas could take months, with everyone crowded closely together. They weren't fed well, and they didn't sleep well. When the weather was stormy, the ship would rock on the waves. Phillis was such a young girl, and she had been taken away from her family. She had no idea where she was going or what her life would be like when she got there.

VOYAGE TO AMERICA

The trip took so long to cross the ocean and the people taken from Africa were treated so poorly that some of them didn't even live to see America.

~

Slaves worked very hard on board the slave ships that brought them to America.

An illustration of a typical slave auction

Slave Auction

It was 1761 when Phillis came to America. When the ship arrived, it landed in Boston. This is the biggest city in Massachusetts, which was then a **colony** and is now a state. When Phillis got off the ship, she was taken to be sold at an **auction**.

At a slave auction, buyers wanted to see these people who had been taken from Africa. Buyers would look to see how strong the Africans were, how healthy, and how hard they were likely to work. The harder the buyer would be able to work a slave, the more a buyer would pay for him or her.

BIDDING AT AUCTIONS

There are no price tags at an auction. Instead, one person says how much he will pay for something. If others will pay more, they say so. This is called "bidding." Whoever will pay the most is called "the highest bidder" and becomes the buyer.

~

A mother and her daughter are sold at auction.

The Wheatleys

★

Many people were bought by buyers who would treat the slaves no better than animals and work them so hard they'd get hurt. Phillis was lucky. The family that bought her was named the Wheatleys. John Wheatley was a tailor who made clothes, and his wife, Susannah, was a loving mother to their two children. The Wheatleys had a lot of money and lived in a nice house.

Maybe they felt sorry for the little African girl, who had turned eight years old. The Wheatleys knew the little girl wouldn't be able to work as hard as the men who were sold at the auction, but she was the one they bought. They brought her home and treated her almost as if she was their own daughter. They gave her the name "Phillis Wheatley."

PHILLIS OR PHYLLIS?

Today this name is usually spelled "Phyllis," but back then it was often spelled "Phillis," which is how the Wheatleys spelled it. Some books now refer to her as "Phyllis Wheatley."

~

Letting Her Learn

★

Instead of making her work all the time, the Wheatleys let Phillis learn how to read and write. Her main teacher was Mary Wheatley, daughter of John and Susannah.

Phillis quickly showed that she was really smart. Mary taught Phillis to read the Bible and to read the work of famous poets. Phillis was a really good reader by the time she was 12. Before long, Phillis began to write her own poems.

TUTORS

Tutors are like teachers, but rather than having a whole class of students, they usually teach one student at a time. Some tutors teach only one subject, like reading or arithmetic.

~

One of the poets Phillis liked to read: John Milton

Reverend George Whitefield, the subject of Phillis's elegy

The Poems of Phillis Wheatley

At the age of 13, Phillis wrote her first poem. Since she'd learned to read from the Bible and from reading famous poets who wrote about religious subjects, many of Phillis's poems were also about religion.

In 1770, when Phillis was only 17, she wrote a poem that people all over Boston and Massachusetts thought was really good. It was titled "On the Death of the Rev. Mr. George Whitefield, 1770." It was about the death of a minister that a lot of people had loved. The poem showed how sad people were that the Reverend Whitefield had died.

The poem was printed not only in Boston, but also was published in Philadelphia and as far away as London, England. At the time, many people thought that African Americans weren't as good as white people and that they weren't smart enough to be great writers. While still a young girl, Phillis showed she was a good writer.

ELEGY

An elegy is a type of poem written to celebrate the life of someone who has recently died. The poem that made Phillis famous was an elegy.

~

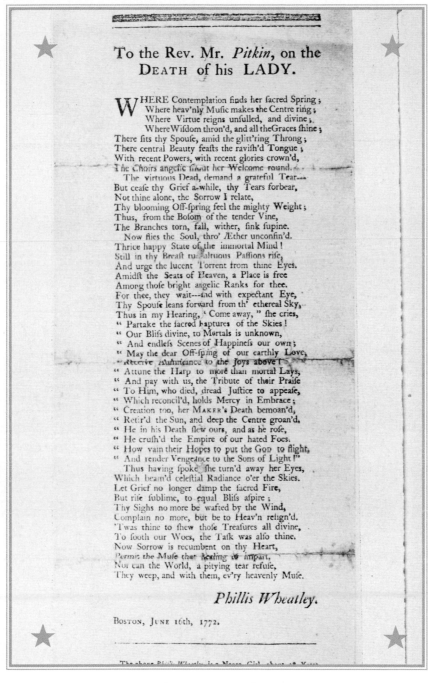

To the Rev. Mr. *Pitkin*, on the DEATH of his LADY.

WHERE Contemplation finds her sacred Spring;
  Where heav'nly Music makes the Centre ring;
  Where Virtue reigns unsullied, and divine;
    Where Wisdom thron'd, and all the Graces shine;
There sits thy Spouse, amid the glitt'ring Throng;
There central Beauty feasts the ravish'd Tongue;
With recent Powers, with recent glories crown'd,
The Choirs angelic shout her Welcome round.
  The virtuous Dead, demand a grateful Tear---
But cease thy Grief a-while, thy Tears forbear,
Not thine alone, the Sorrow I relate,
Thy blooming Off-spring feel the mighty Weight;
Thus, from the Bosom of the tender Vine,
The Branches torn, fall, wither, sink supine.
  Now flies the Soul, thro' Æther unconfin'd.
Thrice happy State of the immortal Mind!
Still in thy Breast tumultuous Passions rise,
And urge the lucent Torrent from thine Eyes.
Amidst the Seats of Heaven, a Place is free
Among those bright angelic Ranks for thee.
For thee, they wait---and with expectant Eye,
Thy Spouse leans forward from th' ethereal Sky,
Thus in my Hearing, " Come away, " she cries,
" Partake the sacred Raptures of the Skies!
" Our Bliss divine, to Mortals is unknown,
" And endless Scenes of Happiness our own;
" May the dear Off-spring of our earthly Love,
" Receive Admittance to the Joys above!
" Attune the Harp to more than mortal Lays,
" And pay with us, the Tribute of their Praise
" To Him, who died, dread Justice to appease,
" Which reconcil'd, holds Mercy in Embrace;
" Creation too, her MAKER's Death bemoan'd,
" Retir'd the Sun, and deep the Centre groan'd,
" He in his Death slew ours, and as he rose,
" He crush'd the Empire of our hated Foes.
" How vain their Hopes to put the GOD to flight,
" And render Vengeance to the Sons of Light!"
  Thus having spoke she turn'd away her Eyes,
Which beam'd celestial Radiance o'er the Skies.
Let Grief no longer damp the sacred Fire,
But rise sublime, to equal Bliss aspire;
Thy Sighs no more be wafted by the Wind,
Complain no more, but be to Heav'n resign'd.
'Twas thine to shew those Treasures all divine,
To sooth our Woes, the Task was also thine.
Now Sorrow is recumbent on thy Heart,
Permit the Muse that healing to impart,
Nor can the World, a pitying tear refuse,
They weep, and with them, ev'ry heavenly Muse.

            Phillis Wheatley.

BOSTON, JUNE 16th, 1772.

A page from the published elegy

London looked like this in the 1700s, when Phillis lived there.

Published in London

★

In 1773, the Wheatleys took Phillis to London, England. The hard winters in Boston made Phillis feel sick, and the family hoped the trip to a city that is warmer in winter would help her feel better. Her poem had been published there, so Phillis was greeted in London as a great poet.

While she was there, a collection of Phillis's poetry was published in London in 1773. *Poems on Various Subjects, Religious and Moral* made her even better known as a great poet. It was her only collection of poetry published during her life, and the first by an African-American writer.

POETRY

Poetry is a form of writing in which the sound, feeling, and rhythm of the words is as important as the meaning. Often it has a rhyme at the end of a line (though not always).

~

A Free Woman

★

When Phillis returned to America, she was no longer a slave. The Wheatley family gave her **freedom**. In 1778, she married an African American named John Peters. They had three children.

Phillis continued to write. She wrote about how slavery was wrong. And she wrote a letter to George Washington, who had led the army to victory in the Revolutionary War and had become the first president. President Washington wrote her back, saying she had "great poetical talents."

Young slaves often served in white people's houses.

George Washington on his estate

Freed slaves learn to read.

Her Poetry Lives On

On December 5, 1784, Phillis died in Boston. She was only 31 years old. Times were very hard in those days for African Americans, and she and John didn't have very much money. The family was poor, but they were free.

Her poetry became even more famous after her death. A lot more people began to believe that slavery was wrong, and they read Phillis's poetry as proof that an African American should have as much freedom as a white American. Today we remember Phillis as a great poet, and a great hero.

Time Line

1753 ★ Phillis Wheatley is born.

1761 ★ Phillis comes to America.

1770 ★ "On the Death of the Rev. Mr. George Whitefield, 1770" is published.

1773 ★ Phillis goes to England and is greeted as a great poet.

1773 ★ *Poems on Various Subjects, Religious and Moral* is published.

1778 ★ Phillis marries John Peters.

1784 Phillis dies in Boston at the age of 31.

Glossary

African Americans (AF rih kun uh MERuh kunz) — Americans of darker skin whose ancestors came from Africa

auction (OK shun) — a sale in which items are sold to those willing to bid the most money

colony (KOL uh nee) — a territory ruled by another country

continent (KONT un unt) —a large mass of land, usually with more than one country

freedom (FREE dum) — the state of being free

kidnapped (KID NAPT) — taken away by force

poetry (PO uh tree) — a form of writing that often (but not always) has lines that rhyme

slavery (SLAYV uh ree) — the ownership of one human being by another, now outlawed in the United States and most of the world

tutors (TOOT urz) — personal teachers, who often work with one student on one or more subjects

Index

Africa   8, 11, 12, 15

African Americans   4, 7, 8, 22, 26, 29

Boston, Massachusetts   15, 22, 25, 29

Civil War   11

elegy   22

London, England   22, 25

"On the Death of the Rev. Mr. George Whitefield, 1770"   21

Peters, John   26, 29

Poems on Various Subjects, Religious and Moral   7, 25

poetry   7, 25, 29

Revolutionary War   4

slaves, slavery   4, 11, 26

Washington, George   26

Further Reading

Burke, Rick. *Phillis Wheatley*. Heinemann Library, 2003.

Egan, Tracie and J. T. Moriarty. *Phillis Wheatley: African American Poet = Poeta Afroamericana*. The Rosen Publishing Group, Incorporated, 2003.

Kent, Deborah. *Phillis Wheatley: First Published African-American Poet*. The Child's World, Incorporated, 2003.

Websites to Visit

http://earlyamerica.com/review/winter96/wheatley.html

http://www.lib.udel.edu/ud/spec/exhibits/treasures/american/wheatley.html

http://www.uoregon.edu/~rbear/wheatley.html

About the Author

Don McLeese is an award-winning journalist whose work has appeared in many newspapers and magazines. He earned his M.A. degree in English from the University of Chicago, taught feature writing at the University of Texas and has frequently contributed to the World Book Encyclopedia. He lives with his wife and two daughters in West Des Moines, Iowa.